Understanding Cryptocurrency

John Levite

ISBN: 9798848341973

DEDICATION

I dedicate this book to the Almighty God and my mentor Rapostle Sam.

DISCLAIMER

Past performance may not be indicative of future results. The information contained in this book and the resources available shall not be understood or construed as financial advice. I am not an attorney, accountant or financial advisor nor am I holding myself out to be and the information contained in this book is not a substitute for financial advice from a professional who is aware of the facts and circumstances of your individual situation.

CONTENTS

INTRODUCTION

No one dives into the crypto space without a trading platform, for you to trade crypto you need a trading platform in which I recommend Binance as my trading platform.

To trade on BINANCE you need to follow this simple steps. Let's get started in 5 quick and easy steps:

1. Register Account

2. Complete Verification

3. Deposit Crypto

4. Buy Crypto

5. Explore Binance Products

Step 1: Register Account

Register a Binance account from the <u>Binance app or website</u> with your email or phone number.

Step 2: Complete Verification

You can complete Identity Verification on your Binance account to unlock the fiat deposit and withdrawal limits. This process typically takes a few minutes to complete, which includes verifying your basic account information, providing ID documentation, and uploading a selfie/portrait.

Be sure to secure your Binance account - while we do everything to keep your account secure, you also have the power to increase the security of your Binance account. See our Security Tips for more information.

Step 3: Deposit Crypto:

If you already hold crypto in another wallet, you can deposit them into your Binance Wallet.

Step 4: Buy Crypto Deposit Fiat

Depending on your country, you can deposit up to 50+ fiat currencies, such as EUR, BRL, and AUD,NGN to your Binance account using bank transfer and bank cards. Once deposited, you can use them to buy crypto directly. Buy Crypto Using P2P (Peer-to-Peer) you can buy crypto with P2P methods, too. This allows you to buy crypto from other crypto enthusiasts like you directly. Visit this page to learn more on how to buy crypto on P2P.

CHAPTER 1

UNDERSTANDING CRYPTOCURRENCY

Everybody reading this book must have heard about Bitcoin but don't know much about bitcoin or wanting to know more, this is known as the alpha Coin, the first Crypto ever to be traded, it was released in 2009; however, the only coin that was in existence as at that time was bitcoin and wasn't tradable until after other Crypto begin to surface. To the question, what is crypto-trading? Crypto-trading is simply buying one Crypto with another, with the hope that the coin will increase in value. Trading also means buying and selling, so we can also say that Crypto trading is the buying and selling of Cryptocurrency for profit maximizing (you buy when it's low and sell when it's high); Today cryptocurrency trading has now become popular in different countries, however the popularity in crypto doesn't substitute acquiring the right knowledge because even the skilled in cryptocurrency trading make losses how much more someone who doesn't have the right knowledge; experienced traders use lots of different trading tools to help them pick the right coins at the right time. This can include software that helps investors analyze previous pricing trends etc. Nevertheless, everyone must start somewhere! As long as you are not trading more than you can afford to lose, there is no harm in giving it a trial.

There are two types of Traders

1. Short term traders

2. Long term traders

Short-Term Traders:

Short-term traders are those who buy cryptocurrency but only plan to hold on to it for a short amount of time. This can be anything from minutes, hours, days, weeks or even a few month(s)

Long-Term Traders

The word **"HODL"** is mostly used by long term traders. It's a commonly used term in Crypto space, if you are just hearing it, it means you are completely new to the crypto space, it's not an English word that is found in the dictionary, but you'll certainly find it in crypto groups and communities. **"HODL"** is a slang word meaning to hold a cryptocurrency long term rather than selling it. Its actual meaning is **"Hold On for Dear Life"**. Usually, long-term crypto trading means to hold a coin for one year or more. Let's take for example, Bitcoin was sold in 2017 for $0.35 and peradventure you bought $10 worth of it, you will be having 28 units of it, now imagine you are still holding this coin by now you will be having about $1.6m; but who has that kind of patience. **N.B** - Whenever you are trading whether longer term traders or short term traders, you must have it in mind that it is possible to lose your entire investment especially if you don't have the right mentorship and the right attitude towards cryptocurrency – Put yourself together as you journey through this book to learn all that you need to do to trade like a pro and make more than you can possibly lose. "The cryptocurrency market is very volatile, and although some people have made lots of money, lots of people have lost money too. You should never trade with any amount that you can't afford to lose. - anonymous" One thing you must also take note is not to be carried away with the hype of certain coins on social media or YouTube influencers because some of them are been paid to promote their coin name which may cause a temporal increase in the price and enter into the trade for the fear of missing out **(FOMO)**.

WHAT IS CRYPTOCURRENCY?

Cryptocurrency is a digital asset which you can use as a means of transaction, they have an online ledger with a strong cryptography which can be used to secure online transactions. Cryptocurrency are an alternative to traditional money. Today, some companies accept cryptocurrency as a form of payment. Meanwhile, they look a lot like other asset classes because they are intangible and extremely volatile. Many companies have issued their own currencies, often called tokens, and these can be traded specifically for the good or service that the company provides. Cryptocurrency works using a technology called blockchain. Blockchain is a decentralized technology spread across many computers that manages and records transactions. There are over 9000 Crypto on coinmarketcap.com (a market research site) which are tradable on different exchange sites like Binance, Okex, crypto.com, coinbase etc… The total value of all cryptocurrency on April 13, 2021, was more than $2.2 trillion, according to CoinMarketCap, and the total value of all Bitcoin, the most popular digital currency, was pegged at about $1.2 trillion.

Top (5) Cryptocurrency by MARKET CAP as at 10th of May 2021

1. Bitcoin $1.1trn

2. Ethereum $477bn

3. Binance $404bn

4. Doge coin $69.28bn

5. Cardano $57.9bn

HOW SOME PEOPLE SEE CRYPTOCURRENCY

- Some people see Cryptocurrency as the future of money and have been rushed by many in the world even before they become more valuable.

- Some people see it as a means whereby central authorities will not have control over the supply of money since the central authorities have been able to reduce the value of money via inflation.

- Some see Crypto as an opportunity to save and have it increased in the future. Since bank savings reduces your funds and doesn't add up value; instead of that it reduces your chances of increasing your assets in the bank. Since crypto assets is affected by demand and supply a proper technical analysis goes a long way and have a lot of impart on assets acquired – these has now made cryptocurrency another form of business and not a side hustle.

Cryptocurrency can act like real money—in a sense,

they are real money—but they take a digital monetary form and are not managed or governed by any central authority. A true product of the digital age, cryptocurrency operate without the involvement of banks, governments, or any middleman. However, in most cases you will need to use a digital currency exchange to buy and sell cryptocurrency which I will be discussing in a latter chapter. What provides security is that cryptocurrency are encrypted (secured) with specialized computer code called cryptography. They're designed like a complicated puzzle on purpose so that they're hard to crack (and hack). By September 2020, the number of blockchain wallet users rose to more than 50 million, according to research published by Statista —with Bitcoin boasting more than 7 million active users - sofi.com legendary investor Warren Buffett also compared Bitcoin to paper checks: "It's a very effective way of transmitting money and you can do it anonymously. Bitcoin as the currency of the future, it should be noted that a currency needs stability so that merchants and consumers can determine what a fair price is for goods. Bitcoin and other cryptocurrency have been anything but stable through much of their history. For example, while Bitcoin traded at close to $15,000 in December 2017, its value then dropped to as low as about $3,200 a year later. By December 2020, it was trading at record levels again, the price was ranging from $20,000 - $25,000 and in 2021 currently trading at $47,000, over the years bitcoin and other cryptocurrency have proven to be the best form of investment so far in the history of the world; this price volatility creates a dilemma. If bitcoin might be worth a lot more in the future, people are less likely to spend and circulate them today, making them less viable as a currency but rather an investment. Why spend a bitcoin when it could be worth three times the value next year? Are cryptocurrency legal? There's no question whether they're legal or illegal it depends on the policy of the country where cryptocurrency is been traded, However, In Nigeria the Central Bank of Nigeria has banned her bank from its use, meaning that Nigerian crypto enthusiasts may have problem as regards the trading of cryptocurrency within the region of Nigeria, However, In Nigeria Cryptocurrency remains a legal asset.

HOW TO BUY CRYPTOCURRENCIES

To buy cryptocurrency, you'll need a "wallet," an online app that can hold your currency. Generally, you create an account on an exchange, and then you can transfer fiat (real) money to buy cryptocurrency such as Bitcoin or Ethereum.

How do I build my portfolio against 2022?

Your strategy will guide your portfolio. And similar to purchasing something new like an automobile, you first look and study the different models to identify which one suits your requirements best. The level of due diligence you will need is similar to when you are considering investing in other financial asset. Although it all depends on your particular expectations regarding the assets and coins to include in your portfolio, below, we look at several Cryptocurrency trading pointers that will give you a head start as you venture into the fast-paced cryptocurrency trading space.

Understand Cryptocurrency Basics

The fact that you are perhaps only making a small investment or financial allocation to a cryptocurrency like Bitcoin doesn't mean homework is not needed on your part before you buy or invest. You should first endeavor to understand and apply the basic principles of digital assets and blockchain technology. When entering into the crypto trading space, the venture should be approached with a long-term mentality to be profitable. At the same and social media should give you an idea of how the community is engaging and how the particular coin is performing. A coin should not be the only one that needs a strong community, as an individual you need a community of traders to help you with information: what learning from YouTube will not give you is a strong crypto-community and a hand on mentorship guidance.

CHAPTER 2

HOW TO DO YOUR OWN RESEARCH

Cryptocurrency is not a lazy man's work it requires a lot of hard work and dedication, it requires brain work and heart work; In cryptocurrency you must understand that your emotional stability is also important, you have to conduct a heart check before analyzing your portfolio, the concept of crypto emphasis on personal research irrespective of who gives you signal, which signal channel you subscribed to, you must be aware that any market you enter without an analyses is pure gamble, my mentor has this to say "Cryptocurrency is not an escape route from hard work as man think but an embrace of smart work. This doesn't mean, the mind isn't productive. The truth is you will need to do research, understand crypto beyond buying and selling and delve deep into DeFi, Blockchain and many more, those who see crypto as a lazy man's investment that requires no work are simply ignorant, at best. There is work to do but once you've done it, there's a lot of rest that crypto will give to you" – Rapostle Sam.

There are questions that you must ask and research about:

1. Who owns the company? An influential and a person of integrity, as the owner is a good sign for any project.

2. Who are those investing in the project is an important question to ask? It's a good sign if other influential investors want a piece of the project.

3. Based on the research done would you own a stake in the company or just currency or tokens? Owning a stake means you get to participate in its earnings

(you're an owner), while buying tokens simply means you're entitled to use them, like chips in a casino.

4. Is the currency already developed, or is the company looking to raise money to develop it? The more detailed it has, the better your chances it's legitimate. But even legitimacy doesn't mean the currency will succeed. That's an entirely separate question to ask.

Consider Why You Are Investing in Cryptocurrency

According to Investopedia, Perhaps the most fundamental question you should ask yourself before making a cryptocurrency investment is why you're doing it. There are series of investment opportunities available in the world today (many of which offer more stability and less risk than digital currencies). Are you interested simply because of the trend or crazy profits been made? Or is there a more compelling reason for an investment in one or more specific digital tokens? Of course, different investors have various personal investment goals, and exploring the cryptocurrency space may make more sense for some individuals than for others.

Another important aspect to consider is **TIMING** on one hand, buying into a hot new currency before it explodes in popularity and value may prompt investors to move equally quickly. In actuality, though, you're more likely to see success if you monitor the industry before making a move. Cryptocurrency tend to follow particular price patterns. One of the most important investment policy is to manage risk and maximizing profit; the global crypto market runs 24x7 with equal access to all investors without a bias for geography or nationality unless your country has set a ban that works against the adoption of crypto assets; For those ready to dip their toes into the cryptocurrency world, discerning the best time to invest is key. The crypto market is notoriously volatile with as much as 30 per cent difference in prices within a day. However, managing risk is possible and within everyone's reach. We continue to advise investors to only invest a minor share of the overall portfolio or not to invest more than what they can afford to lose. Strategies vary according to individual goals and risk appetite but the following approach works in general even for amateurs.

GET RID OF GET RICH QUICK MENTALITY

Getting rich over the night is the mindset of an average Nigerian, we want to make money overnight, for example, investing $30 and then waking up to see $10,000 in our portfolio, as much as it is possible, it is not the goal and should not be the goal, this is why a lot of people gets into (FOMO – Fear of missing out) and they end up losing their funds. Building wealth is about patience as much as it is about timing "the entry". In the crypto world, long term investors are more likely to gain wealth than short-term traders. Traders use technical analysis to predict future patterns of a coin depending on its historical performance, trade volumes and other indicators. These indicators, however, serve as a compass. Until the market hits a particular maturity. If you can spot the next altcoin before it rises, you'll have an endless supply of cash, knowledge, and power, you won't be different from Biff Tannen in 'Back to the Future', grasping your own personal copy of Gray's Sports Almanac and predicting altcoin explosions before anyone else.

TWO IMPORTANT STRATEGY

1. THE OBVIOUS STRATEGY

I call it **THE OBVIOUS STRATEGY** because every trader should know about this without anyone telling them; the best way to understand altcoin, and to come close to predicting them, is to become your own expert. That means diving into every forum, YouTube channel (like Crypto Community), blog post, Telegram channels, Twitter feed and every Crypto space you can find. Knowledge truly is power but it can make one weak too, a little miss-interpretation or deception from media could swerve your portfolio into the gutters, Knowledge can be both powerful to you and also dangerous, Knowledge may be light but it can also put you in darkness depending on the kind of knowledge you burst into, you have to understand this at times, you make serious cash with certain money from the same space you got an info from and you can also lose from the same source of information, knowing this will help you and give you a consciousness to vet every information which is known as DO YOUR OWN RESEARCH (DYOR). The more you can spot buzzwords, coded languages on different platforms, the easier it will be to separate the shills from the experts. Any outstanding claim requires equally outstanding evidence, so while there's no singular forum you can find that 99% of the crypto world doesn't know about, you can create that forum in your own mind by discerning what's valuable, what garbage is, and what's worse than garbage.

2. THE NOT-SO OBVIOUS STRATEGY

This answer may not tickle your pickle in the way you'd hoped, but it's worth mentioning, everyone wants positive answer at all times but you must also learn that theirs a way you can begin swimming from deepest part of the ocean and not from the top. And by that I mean, chasing the "next big thing" isn't always the right approach if you want to grow your knowledge and wealth. Looking for the next 50x or 100x project can be a thrill, but wading through those initial pumps can leave you with nothing. It's missing the forest for the trees. With a seemingly endless supply of altcoin spewing into the market, the vast majority are meme coins, scams, pump and dump schemes, or rug pulls, trying to turn $10 into $500 in the short-term is exciting, but not always ideal, Take your $10 and use it to build long-term wealth by looking for solid fundamentals. Even if you're chosen altcoin has already been found, that doesn't mean it can't become a valuable addition to your crypto portfolio and help you accumulate wealth over time.

DOWNLOAD THE FOLLOWING MOBILE APPS

Under this segment I will be explaining how to use one of this apps to do your fundamental analysis.

1. Coin Market Cap

2. Coin Gecko

3. Coin Metrics

4. Trading view

Coin Market Cap

One of the most common activity on CMC is to use it to check crypto rankings but there is more to CMC than just using it to check coin ranking, Meanwhile using CMC does not guaranty 100% profit, every information gotten is based on research methodology of its working personnel, I consider the app to be the world largest leading crypto research app when it comes to analyzing crypto for newbie, it helps you follow your favorite projects and keep track of your investments.

FEW FEATURES TO LOOK UPON

- It helps you to view profit and loss calculations on your top performing assets.

- It has what is called Custom alerts that can help you set alert for any of your favorite project and also to keep your eye on the major crypto you have in your portfolio it's available for IOS and android on playstore.

- Supply: Supply is the number of cryptocurrency coins or

tokens that are publicly available and circulating in the market. The circulating supply of a cryptocurrency can increase or decrease over time. For example, the circulating supply of Bitcoin will gradually increase until the max supply of 21 million coins is reached. Such a gradual increase is related to the process of mining that generates new coins every 10 minutes, on average. Alternatively, coin burn events like the ones performed by Binance, because a decrease in the circulating supply, permanently removing coins from the market. - Binance Academy In other words, the Bitcoin supply is limited to 21 million.

In other words, it is deflationary by nature. As a result, not more than 21 million Bitcoin can ever be mined or be in circulation at any given moment. Other tokens, like Ethereum, have a constant flow of new assets added to the ecosystem, which makes them inflationary. Most cryptocurrency follow a demand and supply principle that determines their growth. So, the question arises: Why are people investing in cryptocurrency with a fixed/limited supply? The supply of a particular cryptocurrency refers to the total number of coins in circulation. Three essential terms relate to supply:

- Fixed supply

Fixed (or maximum) supply is the total number of coins that can ever be in circulation E.g. Bitcoin, Litecoin, Cardano, Stellar, Chain link all have fixed supply

- Total Supply:

Total supply is the number of coins currently mined (including the missing ones that are no longer in circulation or lost).

- Circulating supply:

Circulating supply refers to the total number of coins in circulation.

Relationship between the current value and circulating supply.

There is a strong relationship between the current value and the circulating supply of a cryptocurrency. Bitcoin is by far the world's largest cryptocurrency by market cap, with a fixed maximum supply of 21 million. The reward for mining Bitcoin is reduced by 50 percent every four years.

CHAPTER 3

INVESTMENT RISK POLICY

NEVER and I mean NEVER open a position without a stop loss. If you find yourself getting stopped out too often, it means you are not opening smart trades based on fundamentals and are simply running and gunning. Stop and learn how to trade smartly. It will save you a lot of time and money. - Matt Erman

Should you invest in cryptocurrency in 2022 Or Wait Till 2023?

This is a decision that generally requires a good look at your current financial situation. While you can get started investing in cryptocurrency for just a few dollars, it is easy to get caught up in the excitement of the industry, and the constant FOMO. There are lots of amazing new projects coming out every day, so it is certainly an exciting time to be an investor!

The biggest risks of not investing:

- Losing out to inflation: Inflation is 2%-3% or more in most countries and could go higher. The banks don't pay that much in most countries. Since 2008 and 0% interest rates, many people have indirectly lost over 30% of their money, as this loss to inflation compounds. And one of my major concerns about banks is having to save in the bank and not meet your savings the way you kept them and yet no potential increase of your funds in the bank.

- Currency devaluation: You do manage to beat inflation in bank deposits but you live in a country which experiences a currency shock. This harms expats more than locals, but it can affect everybody, because imported costs associated with a weak currency will eventually push up the inflation rate.

- Institutional risks. The two previous points does sometimes push people towards higher-risk options. Places like Georgia and Cambodia have seen an increase in foreign deposits as both countries offer reasonable deposit rates on the USD. Yet this is taking a risk, for a return which isn't as good as the stock markets relative losses. Let's say you manage to beat inflation in the bank in a safe way, and avoid currency risks. Even in this case, cash has never beaten other investments long-term. If you can deal with a bit of volatility, it makes sense to invest rather than save. You will also feel bad if you have friends who have become wealthy slowly from investing, whilst your money just stays in cash earning 0%.

What is a high-risk investment?

The riskiest type of investment is something that is completely based on speculation. An example is buying and selling crypto without proper analysis whether fundamentals or technical, For example in currency trading. The Euro can't go up against the USD at the same time as the USD goes up against the Euro:

You don't even make any money in the bank holding them. Therefore, it is all about timing, and 99.9% of the people engaging in this activity are speculating. The difference and similarity & signs of a speculator and an investor is:

- They are focusing on hot ideas

- Speculator focus on short-term rather than focusing on the long-term

- Speculator try to buy and sell at market time, as opposed to buying and hodling which is a common feature of an investor.

- Not focusing on diversification at all

- More obsessed with capital appreciation if they are buying property rather than the yield.

- An obsession with stories and personalities, like who the CEO is

- Good investing can be very boring because you will have to take your eyes off your portfolio, it's free of tension.

Much like the traditional equity market, there are always corrections in the cryptocurrency market. Risk management is an effective crypto trading strategy that helps to cut down losses, to help crypto traders from losing all of their money. Corrections in the market are highly evident so it matters how you deal with volatility. While being a successful trader often points to making massive gains, any substantial profit could be lost in just one or two bad trades without proper risk management. Traders who are unsuccessful usually enter a trade without any crypto trading strategies, nor the idea of knowing when to sell for a profit, and how much loss they are willing to risk. While sometimes beginners are able to gamble on a lucky streak in the crypto market, it is unlikely to be able to sustain or maximize profit especially when emotions start to dictate their trades. Successful traders will set their own crypto trading strategies, by planning what price they are willing to pay, and what price they would want to sell to make a profit.

Calculating expected return on investment

The calculation of expected returns is essential, as it forces traders to be able to think through their crypto trades, and select the most profitable ones. Setting stop-loss and take-profit, exit orders are necessary for this calculation. Traders would usually calculate the probability of a gain or loss by using historical data of the cryptocurrency, and breakdowns from the support or resistance levels for more experienced traders, rather than trading on instinct or trending news.

Setting stop-losses and take-profit orders

A stop-loss order is set at a price where the trader will sell a crypto asset to take a loss on the trade — preventing further downside potential to avoid incurring bigger losses. As mentioned, cryptocurrency prices are volatile and are due to retrace at certain times, stop-losses are meant to limit losses before they escalate. A take-profit order is set at a price where the trader will sell a crypto asset to take a profit on the trade.

For more experienced traders, they will try to sell the cryptocurrency before it reaches a resistance level, before the digital asset consolidates again. This could also happen when traders decide to realize their profit, to secure capital gains. Most cryptocurrency exchanges will allow you to be able to set a stop-loss, but at the same time, you will not be able to set a take-profit order, which is an issue. Many experienced traders will do technical analysis on the cryptocurrency, which is based on looking at previous highs and lows — determining the levels of which the crypto price reacts to trend lines on high volume. However, understanding the moving averages and the key levels to trade cryptocurrency is not enough, if you do not have the sufficient tools to manage your trades. Using an automated crypto trading platform is essential to execute your trades effectively, as most exchanges lack efficient tools.

More cryptocurrency investing rules?

Cryptocurrency are a new investment class, with very little data for fundamental analysis or past performance. Here's what to keep in mind when entering this high-risk high-reward space.

1. Don't take very big bets.

The phenomenal returns given by some crypto in the past one year are mouthwatering. Invest only what you are willing to lose Even if you have a high risk appetite, start trading with small amounts. Don't put more than 5% of your overall portfolio in a particular crypto unless you have a capital below $200 asset. After you get familiar with the arena, read up about various coins and understand their value and prospects, before you allocate more.

2. Be ready for extreme volatility

Investing in cryptocurrency is the best way to learn about them. But it is a high-risk high-reward game and you must be able to digest very high volatility. As the crash in May

2021 showed a nightmare fall of 70-80%, there is also a possibility of that repeating itself even in the future. Keep in mind that even the big master like Bitcoin is down 48% from its April high as at the point of writing this book. Enter this market only if you can stomach extreme variations and the implications of an investment going wrong.

3. **Don't act on tips without verifying**

    The crypto space suffers from a severe lack of credible information. Investors are dependent largely on unverified information on social media. Self-styled crypto analysts create Whatsapp groups packed with their accomplices who vouch for their accuracy. These analysts trap gullible investors, first by charging a fee for the tips and then using them for their pump-and-dump operations, I was a victim of one which I will explain in a latter chapter. As a rule, you should verify the information before you invest Check the market cap and trading volumes of the coin. A low market cap and insignificant daily volumes are obvious red flags.

4. **Focus on the big masters**

Like the stock markets, the crypto market has the big masters, mid-caps and shit coins. Don't get tempted into buying shit coins just because you can get a lot of them at a low price. Bigger coins may be costlier but are more stable. In any case, you can buy in fractions so don't worry about the price. Bitcoin is the bluechip of the crypto space and drives the overall market sentiment. Focus on the big master coins like Bitcoin and Ethereum, I will also regard Binance coin as a big master, with some of your money in emerging counters like Solana and Matic. Widely held coins with large market capitalization are less likely to be manipulated than coins that are closely held by a few people.

5. **Ask for help:**

Asking for help from someone who knows what

they are doing, rather than trying to figure it all out on your own, can be the best way for you to learn how to invest properly.

6. **Keep the emotions away from the investment:** Keeping your emotions out of your investment is so important if you want to actually earn money. Emotions get in the way and make it almost impossible to make sound decisions on any of your investments. So you are patience when you are supposed to be greedy and greedy where you are supposed to have patience. Your emotions will cloud your judgment.

7. **Have an exit strategy:** You should make sure that you have an exit strategy right from the beginning. This can help you to keep your emotions out of the game from the beginning and will make it easier for you to stick with your plan rather than losing money. Investing in cryptocurrency can be more financially rewarding, than the risk. With the right crypto index strategy, you can try

to reduce all the risks as much as possible. I believe in the future of cryptocurrency. So the best way to achieve financial freedom through cryptocurrency is to follow the above steps, invest and trade wisely, and you'll achieve your financial goals.

CHAPTER 4

HOW I BANKED MY FIRST $1600

The first time I heard about cryptocurrency was through a friend, while introducing to me about a smart contract called million money, a smart contract MLM business that runs on Ethereum blockchain. The benefit alone was mouthwatering due to my network marketing skills, I ventured into it and then referred up to 35 people on Whatsapp just within the space of one month, I enjoyed doing referral marketing business, this system brought me much gain that during the covid-19 pandemic lockdown I was able to finance myself through the lockdown without struggle; this system was one of the major factor that caused the price increase of Ethereum in 2020, it got to a time when price of Ethereum became so high that the registration fee became unaffordable, so I journeyed away and I discovered a crypto-mining site that will pay 100% ROI on monthly basis this platform has been existing for more than 2 years and so have built enough credibility for me to trust it few month later their system was attacked by cyber fraudsters and it eventually crashed, I was desperate to trade cryptocurrency so I began to search for a mentor, I came across a young man called RAPOSTLE SAM, researched about him to know how genuine he was, and if he had the knowledge I was looking for; after my search I saw him to be the best among other crypto-analyst and crossing his path was divine; he helped me to hit my first $1600, I made so much from his platform and few inevitable loss, I am a conscious follower and student of his, He is the founder of CRYPTO DOMAIN.

In crypto, you have to make conscious decisions, one of which is having a good mentor, the crypto space is an ocean you can't afford to swim alone, and there are various sharks and dangerous "whale" that are ready to devour your portfolio in a matter of seconds. Below are the benefits and dangers of not having someone mentor you.

1. **You have only your own mistakes to learn from:**

sometimes mistakes are the most powerful learning tool you can have. But who says they always have to be your own mistakes? Learning from mistakes your mentor has already made and bounced back from can provide a shortcut on your road to the right decision. There's no road or path you want to cross that someone somewhere hasn't passed through, it also helps you to reap from where you haven't sown. Will their situation always be identical to the ones you will face? NO! But they can allow you to make much more inform decisions. Good mentorship brings about avoidable loss. But lots and lots of people think they can get proper mentorship on YouTube or Facebook. What physical mentorship will give to you YouTube cannot give you.

2. **Quit too early:** you'll quit too early, one of the valuable lessons, I learnt from Rapostle is the never quit principle, His story kept me going even though there was loss, How that sometimes the funds meant for personal

upkeep was invested and yet he wasn't getting returns.

You see when crypto throws you a stone, you are likely

never going to recover, if you don't have a mentor

"you're a lone ranger in a deadly forest without an aid".

3. **Sense of Achievement:** The achievement of your

mentor is enough to work you through into your own

success story; His success means you can also do it,

Motivation is part of what helps you sustain and to have

a sound mind. I've learnt a lot in the last year especially

in 2021, having a guide is one of them, you can't have a

good guide and get it all wrong, been a mentee means

you are a student and a student pays his teachers per

profit in crypto – its equal to semester, a student listens

to his teachers, a student reports back to his teachers, a

student does not double date, that is, having two

mentors – this is why you must vet him well before

asking him to journey with you on the road to stardom.

There are those who are where you are going to, finding

and sticking to them is a major way of building a wealth

structure in this crypto space.

CHAPTER 5

CRYPTOCURRENCY COMMON TERMINOLOGIES

1. **Address**:

In digital currency, an address is basically a destination where a user sends and receives digital currency. These addresses usually include a long series of letters and numbers, just like your bank account have account number so also, your wallet have addresses that are distinguish to you alone. Note: The bitcoin wallet on your Binance is not the same with the one on Okex likewise your wallet address is not the same with the one on trust wallet, different exchanges, different wallet addresses, you have to note, an error in your wallet address generation can cause loss of asset for life no matter the amount even if its $100,000,000.

2. **Altcoin**:

An altcoin is a digital currency other than bitcoin. There are more than 1,000 altcoin listed on data source CoinMarketCap presently. Another way of describing the term "altcoin" is referring to it as an alternative protocol asset, meaning that it follows a protocol (set of rules) that's different from that of bitcoin. Ethereum is an altcoin, Tron is an altcoin, Win, Kp3r, Uniswap, BNB etc.... every coin aside bitcoin is an altcoin.

3. Arbitrage

In crypto, arbitrage refers to taking advantage of the price difference between two different exchanges. If bitcoin is selling for $8,950 on one exchange and $9,000 on another, a trader can buy the digital currency on the first exchange and sell it on the second for a modest profit. You have to be careful of network charges when trying this strategy, in trying to make profit you can make loss.

4. ATH:

"ATH" is an abbreviation of "all-time high." This term can be quite helpful to know for tracking the digital currency markets. These assets are so volatile, so keeping their ATH in mind can prove valuable. A digital currency could potentially hit several local highs before rising to a new all-time high. I researched a coin whose ATH is $600 and this coin dropped down to $200, I checked on the coin, the yearly chart, weekly, supply and the trading volume and I discovered it's a good coin to buy, I invested in the coin and in less than a month I doubled my investment, any trade you fail to analyze before trading is gamble.

5. **Bear/Bearish:**

If a trader thinks a cryptocurrency will depreciate, their sentiment surrounding the digital asset is "bearish." In many situations, traders will make use of this expectation by taking a short position on an asset, meaning that they will make a wager that will pay off should the asset in question fall in value. When you study the life of a bear they fight from the standing position and fall on their prey with the intention of using her claws as a major weapon to fight from the upward position down to the ground.

6. **Bull/Bullish:**

When an investor has this optimistic expectation of an asset's increase in overtime, this frame of mind is described as "bullish."

7. **Fiat Currencies:**

Fiat currencies are currencies that have value because they are minted by a central bank. Fiat means "by decree," and these currencies have value because some central authority has decreed that they have monetary value. Examples of fiat currencies include the Nigerian naira, the British pound, euro and Japanese yen, what you regard as paper money is referred to as fiat currency.

8. **FOMO:**

The term "FOMO" stands for the phrase "fear of missing out." This occurs when investors start buying up a particular asset based on their expectations that it will rise in value. Market participants can easily flock to an asset should that asset experience sharp gains. Getting caught up in

FOMO can be dangerous. More specifically, buying up an asset because it has recently enjoyed some notable upside can cause one to fall victim to market manipulation. if you get caught up in this you will lose a lot, greediness is what affect people here, when a coin begins an upward movement, people want to buy and get into the market but what I want to do is stay out.... big mistake is to buy an asset (coin) when on the uptrend especially when it moves above the 60 radar in the RSI chart of that particular coin. The fact about this is 50/50 it can either go up if you are lucky but most times you come back with a loss.

9. **FUD**:

Fear, uncertainty and doubt can be summed up using the term "FUD." The idea behind this is that market participants may spread misleading or inaccurate information in order to cause an asset's price to decline. A trader may want an asset's price to fall so they can either short it successfully or buy in at a lower price and increase their chance of generating a gain.

10. HODL:

Cryptocurrency investors developed the term "HODL," which stands for "hold on for dear life." The acronym originally came from a misspelling of the world "hold." Digital currencies can be highly volatile, so when they start experiencing significant price fluctuations, some market participants state that they should simply "HODL." Cryptocurrency investors developed the term "HODL," which stands for "hold on for dear life." The acronym originally came from a misspelling of the word "hold."[9] Digital currencies can be highly volatile, so when they start experiencing significant price fluctuations, some market participants state that they should simply "HODL." Some bought bitcoin in 2009 when it was first mined and some got it almost for free. One of the safest way to gain in crypto is to buy and hold a coin on long term basis, trading can cost you due to market volatility.

11. **ICO**:

An initial coin offering (ICO) represents the first time that an organization offers digital tokens to the public in an effort to raise money. Companies frequently hold these offerings so they can finance projects.

12. **IPO:**

These digital token sales have often been likened to initial public offerings (IPOs), where companies sell more traditional assets such as stocks and bonds in order to raise money. some of us will be familiar especially airdrop lovers they tell you to pay certain amount of Ethereum to get probably thousands of their coin which may hit more than a dollar when the coin is launched for use or sale

13. **KYC**:

KYC stands for "know your customer." Many jurisdictions have KYC regulations, which have come to affect startups holding ICOs. These regulations require companies holding these digital token sales to verify the identity of their investor. And am sure we are all familiar with this term KYC; if you have registered on Binance exchange you will know what am saying.

14. **Limit order / limit buy / limit sell:**

Orders placed by traders to buy or sell a cryptocurrency when the price meets a certain amount. They can be thought of as 'for-sale' signs. These orders are what are bought and sold against when traders place market orders. You can decide to place a limit order.... in forex they use the word stop loss.... when you place a limit order, it's an indication of the fact that, you want your order to sell off immediately the price is going beyond the limit you have placed, You can place a trade like that and go to bed knowing that you are on the safer side.... your order will automatically sell off.

15. **Market Cap:**

Market cap is short for market capitalization, which is a term for total market value. The market cap of bitcoin, for example, is the number of BTC outstanding multiplied by the digital currency's price. The term can also be used to refer to a group of digital currencies mining.

16. **Mining:**

Is the process for creating new units of a digital currency. For example, the bitcoin network releases new bitcoin every time a block is mined. In this instance, mining involves confirming transactions and combining them in to blocks. This verification requires hardware and electricity, and miners are rewarded with digital tokens for contributing these needed resources.

17. **Mining Incentive:**

The mining incentive is a reward that miners get for confirming transactions and mining them in to blocks. Verifying the transactions of the bitcoin network, for example, requires specialized hardware and substantial electricity, so miners are compensated with a mining incentive. Initially, bitcoin mining incentive was 50 BTC, but at the time of report, the reward had dropped to 12.5.

18. **Noob:**

Newcomers are frequently described as "noobs" by industry insiders. If you are this person, you may want to sit back and observe before "jumping in with both feet." Digital currencies are highly volatile, so those who are newer to these assets should keep their risky nature in mind.

19. **POS**:

POS stands for "proof of stake," which is another method of confirming transactions. The digital currencies that use this approach to verification frequently provide all their digital tokens up front, and miners are selected based on how many units they have (their stake). In these cases, users who confirm transactions, sometimes referred to as "forgers," receive transaction fees for their contributions.

20. **Private Key**:

A private key is a piece of information— presented as a string of numbers and letters—that an investor can use to access their digital currency.

21. **Public Key:** A public key is an address where an investor can receive digital currencies. This public key, like the private key, is a combination of numbers and letters.

22. **Pump and Dump:**

A "pump and dump" is a type of investment scheme where a market participant—or several—work together to inflate the price of an asset so they can sell it when its value is artificially high. This practice may be particularly pervasive when it comes to digital currencies, as traders can easily get together using Telegram groups with the goal of causing specific cryptocurrency to rise sharply in value.

REFERENCE

- **Duke Preston** licensed financial consultant & generational wealth builder.

- **Rapostle Sam** founder of Crypto Domain, Life Coach, financial Instructor.

- **Investopedia** – the world's leading source of financial content on the web, ranging from market news to investing education.

- **Binance Academy** is a nonprofit blockchain education portal that offers quality, easy to understand content for crypto users and enthusiasts' worldwide.

ABOUT THE AUTHOR

John Levite

He is a business consultant and entrepreneur. The founder and ceo of crypto community and custodian trading concept. He has raised a lot of people in the crypto industry and still raising more. He is a husband and a father. He a pastor in The Levite Family Int'l. He has his national diploma in kwara state polytechnic, Kwara State.

Drop your comment about this e-book: https://tinyurl.com/374rjsva

You can connect with me via:

Whatsapp https://tinyurl.com/4u5nj3km
Facebook https://tinyurl.com/5fzcvvdk